ILLUSTRATIONS

NATIONAL GALLERY OF SCOTLAND

EDINBURGH

PRINTED UNDER THE AUTHORITY OF

HER MAJESTY'S STATIONERY OFFICE

1952

THE SCOTTISH NATIONAL GALLERY COLLECTION includes works in tempera, oil and water-colour, drawings, etchings, engravings, and sculpture. Unless otherwise stated, the pictures reproduced in this book are oil or tempera paintings. The Collection of paintings is fairly fully illustrated, but the few water-colours and drawings included are little more than reminders of the collections from which they are drawn. No engravings or other prints are included.

To make the representation of Scottish Painting as complete as possible, certain pictures, which are of minor importance in themselves, have been included to show the development of the National School.

The illustrations are arranged under the artists' names, alphabetically, save for slight deviations due to the size and shape of the blocks. Measurements are given in inches, height first.

PHOTOGRAPHS

Nearly all the paintings in the Collection have been photographed. Photographic prints are on sale in the Gallery.

REPRODUCTION

Applications for permission to reproduce works in the National Gallery of Scotland should be addressed to the Director.

M18C2O

30 /10/52

Wt. P1561/43   53·885.

AIKMAN, WM.   PORTRAIT OF THE ARTIST.
$29 \times 22\frac{5}{8}$. (167.)

ALEXANDER, R. $31\frac{1}{4} \times 45$. (1648.)   THE HAPPY MOTHER.

ALEXANDER, COSMO JOHN.
ADRIAN HOPE OF AMSTERDAM.
$29\frac{1}{2} \times 24\frac{1}{2}$.   (1882.)

ALEXANDER, JOHN.   PLUTO AND PROSERPINE.
$28 \times 31\frac{3}{4}$.   (1784.)

ALLAN, D.
THE ORIGIN OF PAINTING.
15×12. (612.)

ALLAN, D.   HALKETT FAMILY GROUP.
60¼×94. (2157.)

ALLAN, DAVID.   MRS. TASSIE.
        $29 \times 23\frac{7}{8}$. (415.)

ALLAN, SIR WILLIAM. $12\frac{3}{4} \times 17\frac{1}{4}$. (172.)   THE BLACK DWARF.

AVERCAMP, HENDRICK. WINTER SCENE.
$10\frac{1}{2} \times 16\frac{3}{4}$. (647.)

BAKHUYSEN, LUDOLF. $17\frac{1}{4} \times 23$. (2.) A SQUALL.

BARTHOLOMÉ, P. A.   L'ENFANT MORT.
41 ins. high.   (1543.)

BARYE, A. L.   TIGRE DÉVORANT UNE GAZELLE.
12¾ ins. high.   (1626.)

BASTIEN-LEPAGE, JULES.   PAS MÈCHE.

$52 \times 34\frac{3}{4}$.   (1133.)

BASSANO.   28¼ × 29.   (1635.)
MADONNA AND CHILD WITH ST. JOHN
                    AND DONOR.

BASSANO.   48⅞ × 37¾.   (3.)   A SENATOR.

BASSANO. 70¾ × 92. (100.) THE ADORATION OF THE MAGI.

BLAKE, WILLIAM.   GOD SPEAKING TO JOI
               Water-colour, $15\frac{1}{2} \times 13$.   (2117.)

BLAKE, WILLIAM. THE TRIPLE HECATE.
Water-colour, 16⅜ × 22⅛. (1011.)

BLAKE, WILLIAM. Water-colour, 16 × 13⅛. (R.N. 2281.)
GOD WRITING UPON THE TABLES
OF THE COVENANT.

BONINGTON, R. P.   LANDSCAPE, EVENING.
            Water-colour, $7\frac{1}{8} \times 9\frac{1}{4}$.   (1137.)

        BONINGTON, R. P. $9\frac{1}{2} \times 12\frac{1}{2}$.   (1017.)   LANDSCAPE.

BOUCHER, FRANÇOIS.   MADAME DE POMPADOUR.
13¾ × 17¼. (429.)

BOSBOOM, J.   11⅛ × 16¾. (1468.)   THE PREACHER.

BORDONE, PARIS. $38\frac{1}{4} \times 55\frac{1}{4}$. (10.)   A VENETIAN WOMAN.

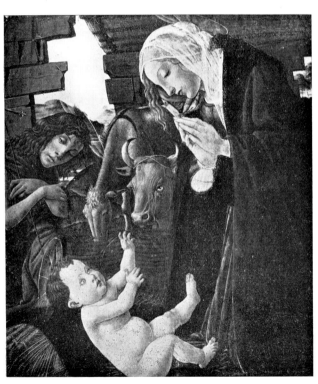

BOTTICELLI (SCHOOL OF). $18 \times 16\frac{1}{4}$. (1536.)
INFANT JESUS IN MANGER, WITH VIRGIN
AND ST. JOHN.

BORGIANNI, O. 40 × 30¼. (48.) ST. CHRISTOPHER.

BOUDIN, L. E. THE PORT OF BORDEAUX.

14⅞ × 24½. (1072.)

B

BOUGH, S.   ROYAL VOLUNTEER REVIEW, AUGUST 7, 1860.
                            $46\frac{1}{2} \times 70\frac{5}{8}$.   (801.)

BRIL, PAUL. $9 \times 11\frac{3}{4}$.   (1492.)   LANDSCAPE.

BRAMANTINO.   SCOURGING OF CHRIST.
13¾ × 9¼.   (1673.)

BRAY, JAN DE.   FOUR PORTRAITS.
(1500-1503.)

BROUGH, ROBERT.   W. DALLAS ROSS, Esq.
$28\frac{1}{4} \times 22\frac{5}{8}$. (938.)

BURNET, J.   AN OYSTER-CELLAR IN LEITH.
$11\frac{3}{8} \times 13\frac{1}{2}$. (1759.)

BURR, A. H.   THE NIGHT STALL.
$20\frac{1}{2} \times 18\frac{1}{2}$. (1000.)

BURR, JOHN.   GRANDFATHER'S RETURN.
$9\frac{3}{4} \times 11\frac{1}{4}$. (1001.)

BUTINONE.
CHRIST DISPUTING WITH THE DOCTORS.
$9\frac{1}{2} \times 8\frac{1}{4}$. (1746.)

CAMERON, HUGH.   GOING TO THE HAY.
$22 \times 16\frac{1}{4}$. (652.)

CAMERON, SIR D. Y.   THE HILL OF THE WINDS.
                46 × 52.   (2080.)

CAMERON, SIR D. Y.   EN PROVENCE.
                31½ × 25¼.   (2081.)

CAMERON, HUGH.   A LONELY LIFE.

33¼ × 25.   (1717.)

CARSE, ALEX.   THE VILLAGE TAILOR.

18⅝ × 24⅝.   (780.)

CASTAGNO (attr.).   THE LAST SUPPER.
                    $10\frac{1}{2} \times 13\frac{3}{8}$.   (1210.)

CATENA.   VENETIAN LADY.
                    $13\frac{3}{4} \times 10\frac{1}{2}$.   (1675.)

CARDUCHO, V.   DREAM OF S. HUGH.
$22\frac{3}{4} \times 18.$ (459.)

CHALMERS, G. P.   MODESTY.
$25 \times 18\frac{3}{4}.$ (1477.)

CHARDIN, J-B. S. VASE DE FLEURS.
$17\frac{1}{4} \times 14\frac{1}{4}$. (1883.)

CIMA. MADONNA ENTHRONED.
$18\frac{3}{4} \times 15\frac{1}{2}$. (1190.)

CHARDIN. $15\frac{1}{2} \times 12\frac{1}{2}$.   (959.)   STILL LIFE.

CLEEF, JOOS VAN.   DEPOSITION FROM THE CROSS.

Centre, 42×28 ; sides, $43 \times 12\frac{1}{2}$.   (1252.)

CLOUET, JEAN.
MADAME DE CANAPLES.
$13\frac{1}{2} \times 10\frac{5}{8}$. (1930.)

CORNELISZ, J.   CRUCIFIXION.
$10\frac{1}{4} \times 7\frac{3}{4}$. (1253.)

CONSTABLE, JOHN.   THE VALE OF DEDHAM.
                        $55\frac{1}{2} \times 48$.   (2016.)

CONSTABLE, JOHN. ON THE STOUR.
            $7\frac{5}{8} \times 8\frac{7}{8}$.   (1219.)

COROT. THE ARTIST'S MOTHER.
$15\frac{1}{2} \times 12\frac{3}{8}$. (1852.)

COROT. LANDSCAPE WITH CASTLE.
$15\frac{3}{4} \times 21$. (1449.)

COROT.   THE GOATHERD.
$23\frac{1}{2} \times 19\frac{1}{4}$.   (1447.)

COROT.   ENTRÉE DU BOIS.
$17\frac{5}{8} \times 13\frac{5}{8}$.   (1681.)

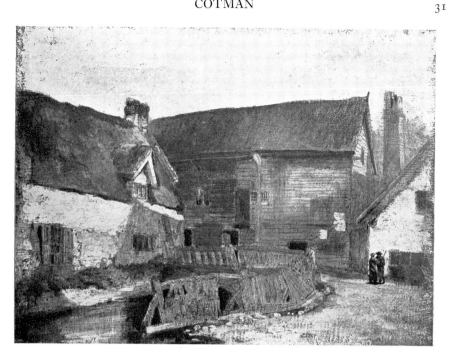

COTMAN, J. S.   13½ × 17⅞. (960.)   LAKENHAM MILLS.

COTMAN, J. S.   BUILDINGS ON A RIVER.
13¾ × 11¾. (931.)

C

COTMAN, J. S.   CASTLE EDEN DEAN.
Water-colour, 16⅝ × 14¾. (1025.)

COTMAN, J. S.   A SHADY POOL—
WHERE THE GRETA JOINS THE TEES.
Water-colour, 17⅜ × 13⅜. (1136.)

CRANACH, LUCAS. VENUS AND CUPID.
$14\frac{1}{2} \times 10$. (1942.)

CRAWFORD, E. T. CROSSING THE BAR.
$23\frac{1}{2} \times 35\frac{1}{2}$. (421.)

CRAWHALL, J. STUDY OF A GOAT.
$14\frac{7}{8} \times 16\frac{3}{8}$. (1843.)

CRAWHALL, J. $16\frac{1}{4} \times 16\frac{1}{4}$. (1571.) THE WHIP.

CROZIER, WILLIAM.   EDINBURGH.
$27\frac{1}{4} \times 35\frac{3}{8}$. (1965.)

CROZIER, WILLIAM.   GARDENS IN SNOW.
$27\frac{1}{2} \times 35\frac{5}{8}$. (1976.)

DADDI, BERNARDO.   ALTAR-PIECE WITH WINGS.
Inside mouldings, centre 21 × 11
wings 22 × 6.   (1904.)

FLORENTINE SCHOOL.   BAPTISM AND MARTYRDOM
$7\frac{3}{8} \times 24\frac{1}{8}$.   (1539.)   OF TWO SAINTS.

FLORENTINE SCHOOL.   THE TRIUMPH OF LOVE.
$15\frac{1}{4} \times 55\frac{3}{4}$.   (1940.)

ALOU, AIMÉ-JULES.   DEGAS.   ÉTUDE DE NU.
ins. high.   (908.)   " LAVOISIER."   28 ins. high.   (1624.)

DAUBIGNY, C. F. $14\frac{7}{8} \times 26\frac{1}{8}$.   (1035.)   LA FRETTE.

DAUBIGNY, C. F. COTTAGES AT BARBIZON—EVENING.
$9\frac{1}{4} \times 15\frac{3}{8}$. (1076.)

DAUMIER, HONORÉ. LE PEINTRE.
$10\frac{3}{4} \times 7$. (1616.)

DEGAS, E.   42¾ × 39. (1785.)   DIEGO MARTELLI.

DEGAS, E.   STUDY FOR DIEGO MARTELLI.
                 Drawing, 4⅜ × 6⅝. (R.N. 3873.)

DEELEN, DIRCK VAN.
ARCHITECTURAL SUBJECT.
20⅝ × 18¾. (111.)

DIAZ, N.   18 × 14½. (1454.)   FLOWERS.

DONALD, J. MILNE.   A HIGHLAND STREAM—GLENFRUIN.
$25\frac{1}{2} \times 35\frac{3}{8}$. (987.)

DOUGLAS, SIR W. F. 14×25. (669.)   DAVID LAING, LL.D.

DOUGLAS, SIR W. F. $30\frac{1}{2} \times 61\frac{3}{4}$. (779.)   THE SPELL.

DOUGLAS, SIR W. F.
STONEHAVEN HARBOUR.
$47 \times 23\frac{1}{8}$. (981.)

DOUGLAS, SIR W. F. $5\frac{7}{8} \times 10\frac{7}{8}$.   (973.)   LUNAN BAY.

DOUGLAS, SIR W. F.   HUDIBRAS AND RALPH.
$25\frac{1}{2} \times 41\frac{1}{2}$.   (1479.)

DRUMMOND, JAMES. $43\frac{1}{2} \times 59\frac{1}{2}$. (180.)   THE PORTEOUS MOB.

DRUMMOND, JAMES.
          THE RETURN OF MARY QUEEN OF SCOTS TO EDINBURGH.
                    $34 \times 49\frac{1}{4}$. (625.)

DUNCAN, J. ST. BRIDE.
47½ × 56½. (2043.)

DUPRÉ. A FISHERMAN.
17¾ × 14¾. (1040.)

DUNCAN, THOMAS.
KATHERINE, LADY STUART OF ALLANBANK.
$29\frac{3}{8} \times 24.$ (466.)

DUNCAN, THOMAS.
ANNE PAGE AND SLENDER.
$51\frac{3}{4} \times 40\frac{5}{8}.$ (448.)

DUNCAN, THOMAS.
PORTRAIT OF THE ARTIST.
49¾ × 39⅝. (182.)

DYCE, WILLIAM.   JUDGMENT OF SOLOMON.
59½ × 96½. (521.)

D

DYCE, WILLIAM.   54¼ × 68¼.   (460.)   FRANCESCA DA RIMINI.

DYCE, WILLIAM.   INFANT HERCULES.
35½ × 27⅜.   (184.)

DYCK, ANTHONIS VAN.   92 × 59¾. (119.)   AN ITALIAN NOBLE.

DYCK, ANTHONIS VAN.   MARTYRDOM OF ST. SEBASTIAN.

$88\frac{1}{2} \times 63$. (121.)

DYCK, ANTHONIS VAN. THE LOMELLINI FAMILY.
$104\frac{1}{8} \times 98\frac{1}{4}$. (120.)

DYCK, A. VAN.
STUDY OF A HEAD.
$16\frac{1}{2} \times 14\frac{1}{2}$. (122.)

FAED, JOHN.   THE EVENING HOUR.
13 × 9½. (1142.)

FAED, THOMAS.   EVENING THOUGHTS.
23½ × 17¾. (2136.)

ETTY, WILLIAM.   THE COMBAT.
$99\frac{3}{4} \times 134.$ (189.)

FANTIN-LATOUR, I. H. J. T.   ROSES.
$14\frac{3}{8} \times 15\frac{3}{8}.$ (1455.)

FERGUSON, W. G.   STILL LIFE.

25 × 19½.   (970.)

FLEMISH SCHOOL.   7⅝ × 10⅛.   (1642.)   PIETA.

FLEMISH SCHOOL.
VIRGIN AND CHILD.
$13\frac{1}{2} \times 8$. (1537.)

ICKE,   WILLIAM, THIRTEENTH   FIORENZO DI LORENZO.
RLACH.   BARON GREY DE WILTON.   S. FRANCIS.
           $39\frac{1}{2} \times 29\frac{1}{2}$. (1933.) $13 \times 7\frac{1}{4}$. (1745.)

FLORENTINE ± 1425.   S. FRANCIS.
                        $8\frac{1}{2} \times 12.$ (1540A.)

FLORENTINE ± 1425.   S. ANTHONY ABBOT.
                        $8\frac{1}{2} \times 12.$ (1540B.)

FRASER, ALEXANDER.   HAYMAKING ON THE AVON.
$34\frac{3}{8} \times 46\frac{1}{2}$. (1980.)

FRASER, ALEXANDER.   A GLADE IN CADZOW.
$26\frac{3}{8} \times 35\frac{1}{2}$. (1480.)

FRASER, ALEXANDER. ENTRANCE TO CADZOW FOREST.
$25\frac{1}{2} \times 35\frac{1}{2}$. (1188.)

FRASER, ALEXANDER. A HIGHLAND SPORTSMAN.
$31 \times 43\frac{1}{2}$. (2134.)

FURINI, FRANCESCO. ST. SEBASTIAN.
$19\frac{1}{4} \times 14\frac{3}{4}$. (30.)

GAUGUIN, P. JACOB WRESTLING WITH THE ANGEL.
$28\frac{1}{2} \times 36$. (1643.)

GAINSBOROUGH, T.   MRS. HAMILTON NISBET.
91¼ × 60.   (1521.)

GAINSBOROUGH, T.   THE HON. MRS. GRAHAM.
                    92 × 59½. (332.)

GEDDES, A.   PORTRAIT OF ANDREW PLIMER.
$18\frac{1}{8} \times 15\frac{1}{8}$.   (1847.)

GEDDES, A.   SUMMER.
$29\frac{1}{8} \times 24\frac{1}{8}$.   (191.)

GEDDES, A.   THE ARTIST'S MOTHER.
$28\frac{1}{8} \times 23\frac{1}{8}$.   (630.)

GEDDES, A.   ANNE GEDDES.
49×39.   (2156.)

E

GEIKIE, WALTER. SCOTTISH ROADSIDE SCENE.
16 × 24. (1825.)

GIRTIN, T. GUISBOROUGH PRIORY.
Water-colour, 26 × 19. (1385.)

GOGH, VINCENT VAN. $18\frac{1}{2} \times 24\frac{3}{8}$. (1803.)   LES OLIVIERS.

GORDON, SIR J. WATSON.
RODERICK GRAY, ESQ.
$49\frac{3}{4} \times 39\frac{1}{2}$. (649.)

GOYA.   37¼ × 49. (1628.)   EL MEDICO.

GOYEN, JAN VAN.   DUTCH RIVER SCENE.

16⅜ × 21¾. (1013.)

GOZZOLI (SCHOOL OF).   CHRIST ON THE ROAD TO CALVARY.
$27\frac{1}{2} \times 45\frac{3}{4}$. (953.)

GRAHAM, T.   A YOUNG BOHEMIAN.
$35\frac{1}{2} \times 25\frac{1}{8}$. (957.)

GRAHAM, PETER.　　　　　　　　WANDERING SHADOWS.

51½ × 70½.　(1986.)

GRECO, EL.　　　　　　　　SAINT JEROME.

40 × 37½.　(1873.)

GREUZE, J. B.   GIRL WITH FOLDED HANDS.
$17\frac{5}{8} \times 14\frac{5}{8}$. (437.)

GREUZE, J. B.   BOY WITH LESSON BOOK.
$24\frac{1}{4} \times 18\frac{3}{4}$. (436.)

GREUZE, J. B.   INTERIOR OF A COTTAGE.
24⅞ × 31¾. (37.)

GREUZE, J. B.   GIRL WITH DEAD CANARY.
20¼ × 17¼. (435.)

GUARDI, F.   STA. MARIA DELLA SALUTE.
19 × 15⅛. (1498.)

GUARDI, F.   SAN GIORGIO MAGGIORE.
19 × 15⅛. (1499.)

GUTHRIE,   PORTRAIT OF THE
SIR JAMES.   ARTIST'S MOTHER.
$35\frac{1}{4} \times 27\frac{1}{4}$. (2017.)

GUTHRIE, SIR JAMES. $24\frac{3}{4} \times 36\frac{7}{8}$. (2018.)   PASTORAL.

GUTHRIE, SIR JAMES.   OBAN.
22 × 17¾.   (2087.)

GUTHRIE, SIR JAMES.   THE HIND'S DAUGHTER.
35½ × 29½.   (2142.)

HALS, FRANS.   45¼ × 33½.   (691.)
A DUTCH GENTLEMAN.

HALS, FRANS.   A DUTCH LADY.
45¼ × 33½.   (692.)

HALS, FRANS. VERDONCK.
$18\frac{1}{4} \times 13\frac{3}{4}$. (1200.)

HAMILTON, JAMES. STILL LIFE.
$18 \times 15\frac{1}{2}$. (1833.)

HARVEY, SIR GEORGE.　　　　　　COVENANTERS' COMMUNION.
$30\frac{3}{4} \times 44\frac{3}{4}$.　(608.)

HARVEY, SIR GEORGE.　　$35\frac{1}{2} \times 71\frac{1}{2}$.　(949.)　　　　THE BOWLERS.

HARVEY, SIR GEORGE. $27\frac{1}{4} \times 47\frac{1}{2}$. (919.)   " A SCHULE SKAILIN'."

HEMESSEN, JAN SANDERS VAN.   BACCHUS AND ARIADNE.
$41\frac{1}{8} \times 47\frac{1}{4}$. (78.)

HERDMAN, ROBERT.   45⅜ × 68.   (599.)   AFTER THE BATTLE.

HOBBEMA, MEINDERT.   WATERFALL IN A WOOD.
10⅜ × 8⅝.   (1506.)

HOGARTH, W.   SARAH MALCOLM.
$18\frac{1}{2} \times 14\frac{1}{2}$.   (838.)

HOGARTH, W.   VISCOUNT BOYNE.
$20 \times 14\frac{7}{8}$.   (1657.)

F

HORNEL, E. A.　　　　　$47\frac{5}{8} \times 59\frac{1}{2}$. (1814.)　　MUSIC OF THE WOODS.

HORNEL, E. A.　　KITE-FLYING, JAPAN.
$29\frac{5}{8} \times 18\frac{5}{8}$. (1815.)

HUNTER, GEORGE LESLIE.   REFLECTIONS, BALLOCH.

$24\frac{1}{2} \times 29\frac{1}{2}$. (1794.)

HUNTER, GEORGE LESLIE.   STILL LIFE.

$19\frac{1}{2} \times 23\frac{1}{2}$. (2026.)

JACQUE, C. E.   17½ × 26.   (1457.)   LEAVING THE STALL.

JAMESONE, G.   COUNTESS MARISCHAL.
26½ × 21½.   (958.)

JAMESONE, GEORGE.   ROBERT, MESTER ERSKINE.
$90\frac{1}{2} \times 59$.   (1973.)

JARDIN, KAREL DU.
        HALT AT AN ITALIAN WINE-HOUSE DOOR.
        $31\frac{3}{8} \times 34\frac{5}{8}$. (25.)

KEY, W.   LADY HELEN LESLIE,
                 WIFE OF MARK KERR.
      $15\frac{1}{4} \times 11\frac{1}{4}$. (1939.)

KIDD, WILLIAM. 11⅝×15⅝. (982.) FISHER FOLK

LANCRET, NICOLAS. THE TOY WINDMILL.
19¼ ins. diameter. (440.)

LAUDER, R. S.   29½ × 24½. (1003.)
HENRY LAUDER, BROTHER OF THE
ARTIST.

LAUDER, J. E.
" BAILIE M'WHEEBLE AT
BREAKFAST."
26½ × 19¾. (915.)

LAWRENCE, SIR T.   LADY ROBERT MANNERS.
54¾ × 43½.   (1522.)

LAWSON, C. G.   A SURREY LANDSCAPE.
11⅝ × 9⅝.   (1372.)

LÉGROS, ALPHONSE.   29½ × 37.   (1623.)   THE SERMON.

LÉPINE, S. V. E.   11½ × 20⅝.   (1047.)   LA SEINE À BERCY.

LIEVENS, JAN.   19¾ × 27⅜.   (68.)   A WOODLAND SCENE.

LIEVENS, JAN.   PORTRAIT OF A YOUNG MAN.
                      44 × 38⅛.   (1564.)

LIPPI, FILIPPINO.　　　　　　　　HOLY FAMILY AND ANGELS.
$9\frac{3}{4} \times 14\frac{1}{2}$.　(1758.)

LOCKHART, W. E.　　　　　GIL BLAS.
$59\frac{1}{2} \times 36\frac{3}{4}$.　(945.)

LIZARS, W. H.   23¼ × 26.   (424.)   A SCOTCH WEDDING.

LIZARS, W. H.   20¼ × 25½.   (423.)   READING THE WILL.

LORIMER, JOHN HENRY.   THE ORDINATION OF ELDERS
IN A SCOTTISH KIRK.
43 × 55.   (1879.)

McCULLOCH, HORATIO.   35½ × 59½. (288.)   INVERLOCHY CASTLE.

MACGREGOR, W. Y.   SOUTH OF ENGLAND LANDSCAPE.
15 × 23½. (1694.)

MACGREGOR, W. Y.   A WINTER LANDSCAPE.
34½ × 27¼. (1770.)

MACGREGOR, W. Y. 　　　　　　　　　THE VEGETABLE STALL.
41½ × 59¼. (1915.)

McKAY, W. D. 　　　　　　　　　FIELD WORKING IN SPRING.
25⅛ × 38¾. (1669.)

MACKIE, C. H. THE BATHING POOL.
59 × 58. (2038.)

MACKIE, C. H. " BELVEDERE," VENICE.
27¼ × 34¾. (1732.)

G

MACNEE, SIR DANIEL.   LADY IN GREY.
$49\frac{1}{2} \times 39\frac{3}{8}$.   (1679.)

McKENZIE, ROBERT TAIT.   THE RELAY.
22 ins. high.   (1978.)

McTAGGART, WILLIAM.   MRS. LEIPER.
$29\frac{3}{8} \times 24\frac{1}{2}$.   (1201.)

McTAGGART, WILLIAM.   MACHRIHANISH BAY.
$32\frac{1}{2} \times 48\frac{1}{2}$.   (1906.)

McTAGGART, WILLIAM.   THE COMING OF ST. COLUMBA.
                        50¼ × 80¼. (1071.)

McTAGGART, WILLIAM.   THE YOUNG FISHERS.
                        28⅜ × 42½. (1842.)

McTAGGART, WILLIAM.   HARVEST AT BROOMIEKNOWE.
$34\frac{3}{8} \times 51\frac{1}{4}$. (1907.)

McTAGGART, WILLIAM.   BY SUMMER SEAS.
$17\frac{1}{2} \times 25\frac{1}{2}$. (1483.)

McTAGGART, WILLIAM. $21\frac{1}{4} \times 29\frac{1}{4}$. (1650.)   WHINS IN BLOOM.

McTAGGART, WILLIAM. $47\frac{1}{4} \times 71\frac{1}{4}$. (1834.)   THE STORM.

McTAGGART, WILLIAM. $17\frac{1}{2} \times 23\frac{1}{2}$.   (2137.)   SPRING.

MARTIN, JOHN. 20×28.   (2115.)   MACBETH.

MAES, N.   A DUTCH FAMILY.
       $19\frac{1}{4} \times 14\frac{1}{2}$. (1509.)

MANDER, KAREL VAN.   PORTRAITS.
          $41\frac{7}{8} \times 32$. (824.)

MARIS, J.　　　　$36\frac{1}{4} \times 49\frac{1}{8}$. (1049.)　　　ON THE AMSTEL.

MARIS, J.
SCHEVENINGEN—STORMY WEATHER.
$16\frac{3}{4} \times 11\frac{1}{4}$. (1051.)

MATTEO DI GIOVANNI.   20 × 15½.   (1023.)
MADONNA AND SAINTS.

MELVILLE, A.   ARAB INTERIOR.
37 × 28.   (2144.)

MARIS, J. $13\frac{1}{2} \times 23$. (1050.) AMSTERDAM.

MAUVE, A. THE TOW-PATH—No. 2.
$9\frac{7}{8} \times 7\frac{1}{8}$. (1058.)

MAUVE, A.   A SHEPHERD AND HIS FLOCK.

$14\frac{3}{4} \times 26\frac{1}{8}$. (1068.)

MELVILLE, A. $71\frac{1}{4} \times 76$. (948.)   CHRISTMAS EVE.

MELVILLE, A.   WAITING FOR THE SULTAN.
Water-colour, $21\frac{1}{4} \times 30\frac{1}{8}$.   (1485.)

MELVILLE, A.   A MOORISH PROCESSION.
Water-colour, $23\frac{3}{4} \times 31\frac{1}{2}$.   (947.)

MĚSTROVIĆ, IVAN.

DR. ELSIE INGLIS.

25¾ ins. high. (1214.)

GIULIANO DE' MEDICI,   MICHELANGELO (after)   LORENZO DE' MEDICI,

DUKE OF NEMOURS.   MADONNA AND CHILD.   DUKE OF URBINO.

22 ins. high. (526.)   26 ins. high. (527.)   21½ ins. high. (528.)

MONET, C. POPLARS ON THE EPTE.
$31\frac{1}{4} \times 31\frac{1}{4}$. (1651.)

MONTICELLI, A. $15\frac{1}{4} \times 23\frac{1}{8}$. (1022.) LA FÊTE.

MORE, JACOB.   31 × 38⅞. (1897.)   THE FALLS OF CLYDE.

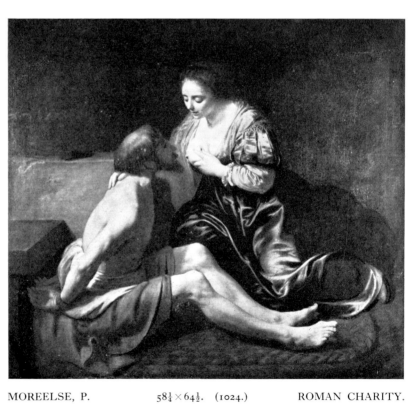

MOREELSE, P.   58¼ × 64½. (1024.)   ROMAN CHARITY.

MORLAND, GEORGE.   THE PUBLIC HOUSE DOOR.
$24\frac{3}{4} \times 30\frac{1}{2}$.   (2015.)

MORLAND, G.   THE STABLE DOOR—A STUDY.
$12\frac{1}{4} \times 14\frac{1}{2}$.   (789.)

H

MORLAND, GEORGE.   THE COMFORTS OF INDUSTRY.
$12\frac{1}{8} \times 14\frac{3}{8}$. (1835.)

MORLAND, GEORGE.   THE MISERIES OF IDLENESS.
$12\frac{1}{8} \times 14\frac{3}{8}$. (1836.)

MUIRHEAD, DAVID.   PORTRAIT OF A LADY.
$29\frac{1}{8} \times 24\frac{1}{4}$. (1765.)

NASMYTH, PATRICK.   AN ENGLISH LANDSCAPE.
14×19. (1894.)

NOBLE, J. CAMPBELL.

SUNSET NEAR GLENCAPLE ON SOLWAY.
$27\frac{1}{2} \times 35\frac{1}{2}$.   (1146.)

NOBLE, ROBERT.   SPRINGTIME, PRESTONKIRK.
$29\frac{1}{8} \times 35\frac{1}{2}$.   (1208.)

OEVER, HENDRICK TEN.   A DUTCH LANDSCAPE.
$26\frac{1}{4} \times 34\frac{1}{4}$. (22.)

ORCHARDSON, SIR W. Q.   MASTER BABY.
$42\frac{1}{4} \times 65\frac{1}{2}$. (1138.)

ORCHARDSON, SIR W. Q.   VOLTAIRE.
                       56 × 78.   (1658.)

ORCHARDSON, SIR W. Q.   THE QUEEN OF THE SWORDS.
                    18⅝ × 31¾.   (1018.)

ORLEY, B. VAN.   BEFORE THE CRUCIFIXION.
25¼ × 32.   (995.)

OSTADE, I. VAN.   SPORTSMEN HALTING.
21 × 23½.   (951.)

PATER, J. B. J. $22\frac{1}{8} \times 27\frac{1}{8}$. (441.)   LADIES BATHING.

PATERSON, JAMES.   EDINBURGH FROM CRAIGLEITH.
                    $26\frac{1}{2} \times 45$. (2023.)

PATON, SIR J. NOEL.   THE QUARREL OF OBERON AND TITANIA.
39 × 60.   (293.)

PATON, SIR J. NOEL.
DAWN : LUTHER AT ERFURT.
$35\frac{1}{8} \times 26\frac{1}{4}$.   (1230.)

PATON, SIR J. NOEL.

THE RECONCILIATION OF OBERON AND TITANIA.

30 × 48¼. (294.)

PERUGINO.   THE COURT OF APOLLO.

28 × 21. (1805.)

PEPLOE, SAMUEL JOHN.   THE BLACK BOTTLE.
$19\frac{1}{2} \times 23\frac{1}{2}$.   (1918.)

PEPLOE, SAMUEL JOHN.   THE GREEN BLOUSE.
$19\frac{5}{8} \times 19\frac{5}{8}$.   (1954.)

PEPLOE, SAMUEL JOHN.   ROSES.
$19\frac{1}{2} \times 23\frac{1}{2}$. (1949.)

PEPLOE, SAMUEL JOHN.   STILL LIFE.
$21\frac{1}{2} \times 19\frac{1}{2}$. (1985.)

PETTIE, JOHN. 16¾ × 20½. (1187.) CROMWELL'S SAINTS.

PHILLIP, JOHN. 56½ × 85½. (836.) LA GLORIA.

PISSARRO, C.   THE MARNE AT CHENNEVIERES.
                    $35\frac{1}{2} \times 56\frac{1}{2}$.   (2098.)

POLIDORO $20\frac{3}{4} \times 26\frac{1}{2}$.   (1931.)   MADONNA.

PRYDE, J.   AN ANCIENT HARBOUR.
24½ × 19½. (2132.)

POUSSIN, N. (after BELLINI).   FEAST OF THE GODS.
68½ × 75¾. (458.)

RAEBURN, SIR H.   92⅝×58½. (623.)   MRS. HAMILTON.

RAEBURN, SIR H.   95 × 59.   (420.)
COLONEL ALASTAIR MACDONELL OF GLENGARRY.

I

RAEBURN, SIR H.
                    MRS. CAMPBELL OF BALLIMORE.
          48¼ × 38½.   (837.)

RAEBURN, SIR H.
                    ALEX. BONAR, ESQ.
          Oval, 26⅞ × 21¾.   (845.)

RAEBURN, SIR H.   PORTRAIT OF THE PAINTER.
$34\frac{1}{2} \times 26\frac{1}{2}$.   (930.)

RAEBURN, SIR H.   MRS. BONAR.
Oval, $26\frac{3}{4} \times 21\frac{7}{8}$.   (846.)

RAEBURN, SIR H.   MRS. SCOTT MONCRIEFF.
$29\frac{3}{8} \times 24\frac{1}{2}$.   (302.)

RAEBURN, SIR H.   LORD NEWTON.
$29\frac{1}{4} \times 24$.   (522.)

RAEBURN, SIR H.   JOHN WAUCHOPE, ESQ., W.S.
30 × 25.   (681.)

RAEBURN, SIR H.
JOHN SMITH, ESQ., OF CRAIGEND.
29 × 24⅜.   (1027.)

RAEBURN, SIR H.   MRS. GEORGE KINNEAR.
34½ × 26¾.   (1223.)

RAEBURN, SIR H.
ADAM ROLLAND OF GASK.
77⅜ × 59⅜.   (822.)

RAEBURN, SIR H. LIEUT.-COLONEL LYON.
$35 \times 26\frac{7}{8}$. (1224.)

RAEBURN, SIR H.
HENRY RAEBURN ON A
GREY PONY.
$13\frac{1}{2} \times 9$. (1026.)

RAEBURN, SIR H.   MRS. KENNEDY OF DUNURE.
$49\frac{1}{8} \times 39\frac{3}{8}$.   (626.)

RAEBURN, SIR H.
DAVID DEUCHAR.
Miniature, $2\frac{3}{8} \times 1\frac{7}{8}$.   (1762.)

RAEBURN, SIR H.   ALEXR. ADAM, LL.D.
49 × 39.   (335.)

RAEBURN, SIR H.
MEDALLION—SIR HENRY RAEBURN.
$3\frac{7}{8} \times 2\frac{3}{4}$.   (1959.)

RAEBURN, SIR H. $86\frac{5}{8} \times 59\frac{1}{8}$.   (1192.)   MRS. FINLAY.

RAEBURN, SIR H.   MAJOR WILLIAM CLUNES.
                   $93\frac{1}{8} \times 59$.   (903.)

RAEBURN, SIR H.   MISS LAMONT OF
29¾ × 24½.   (1878.)   GREENOCK.

RAEBURN, SIR H.   JOHN WAUCHOPE.
30 × 25.   (2149.)

RAEBURN, SIR H. REV. R. WALKER.
29 × 24. (2112.)

RAEBURN, SIR H. ANNE ERSKINE.
30 × 25. (2150.)

RAMSAY, ALLAN.   MRS. BRUCE OF ARNOT.
$29\frac{1}{8} \times 24.$ (946.)

RAMSAY, ALLAN.
JEAN JACQUES ROUSSEAU.
$29\frac{3}{8} \times 24\frac{3}{8}.$ (820.)

RAMSAY, ALLAN.   THE PAINTER'S WIFE.
29¼ × 24¾.   (430.)

RAMSAY, ALLAN.
LADY L. MANNERS, DUCHESS OF
MONTROSE.
29⅛ × 23¼.   (1524.)

RAMSAY, ALLAN. " FLORA MACDONALD."
$29\frac{1}{2} \times 24\frac{1}{2}$. (1884.)

RAMSAY, ALLAN.
JAMES KERR OF BUGHTRIES.
$29\frac{1}{2} \times 24\frac{1}{2}$. (1889.)

RAMSAY, ALLAN.   MRS. DANIEL CUNYNGHAM.
                93 × 57½.   (2133.)

K

RAMSAY, ALLAN.
SIR PETER HALKETT WEDDERBURN.
$29\frac{1}{2} \times 24\frac{1}{2}$.   (1960.)

RAMSAY, ALLAN.   GEORGE BRISTOW.
49×39.   (2119.)

REMBRANDT.   HENDRICKJE STOFFELS.
              $31\frac{1}{4} \times 26\frac{1}{8}$.   (827.)

REYNOLDS, SIR JOSHUA.
          LADY FRANCES SCOTT.
$29\frac{1}{4} \times 24\frac{1}{4}$. (1666.)

REYNOLDS, SIR JOSHUA.
     ADMIRAL VISCOUNT DUNCAN.
$49\frac{1}{8} \times 39\frac{1}{8}$. (1215.)

RICCI, S. AND M. 36⅝×49¼. (7.)
LANDSCAPE WITH GROUPS OF MONKS ENGAGED IN
DEVOTION.

ROBERTI (attr.).
MADONNA AND CHILD WITH ANGELS.
22¾×17¾. (1535.)

ROBERTS, DAVID.
        ROME—SUNSET FROM THE CONVENT OF SAN ONOFRIO.
                  84 × 168.   (304.)

ROCHE, ALEXANDER I.   NELL.
        18⅞ × 16¼.   (1733.)

ROMNEY, GEORGE. 48 × 38½. (1674.)
MRS. WILBRAHAM BOOTLE.

ROSSELLI, COSIMO. ST. CATHERINE OF SIENA.
66½ × 67. (1030.)

RUISDAEL.   THE BANKS OF A RIVER.
52¾×76. (75.)

RUBENS.   S. AMBROSE.
19×14. (2097.)

RUNCIMAN, J. $11\frac{1}{4} \times 8\frac{1}{2}$.   (648.)
THE FLIGHT INTO EGYPT.

RUNCIMAN, A.   LANDSCAPE.
                    $11\frac{1}{4} \times 14\frac{1}{2}$.   (790.)

RUNCIMAN, J.   17 × 23¼. (570.)   KING LEAR.

RUNCIMAN, J.
    CHRIST AND HIS DISCIPLES ON THE ROAD TO EMMAUS.
        6×8. (793.)

SANTVOORT.
THE YOUNG HOUSEKEEPER.
$47\frac{1}{2} \times 35\frac{5}{8}$. (663.)

SAFTLEVEN, H. $29\frac{1}{2} \times 42\frac{1}{2}$. (1508.)   CHRIST PREACHING.

SARGENT, J. S.   LADY AGNEW OF LOCHNAW.
                    49 × 39¼.   (1656.)

SCHÖNFELDT.   BATTLEFIELD—TRUMPETS SOUNDING A RECALL.
                    41 × 90¼.   (85.)

SCOTT, D.   PUCK FLEEING BEFORE THE DAWN.
$36\frac{5}{8} \times 56\frac{1}{2}$. (992.)

SCOTT, D.   THE TRAITOR'S GATE.
$53\frac{7}{8} \times 71\frac{3}{4}$. (843.)

SCOTT, DAVID.   JOHN STIRLING.
        $29\frac{1}{2} \times 24\frac{1}{2}$.   (2073.)

SCOTT, DAVID. $35\frac{1}{2} \times 46\frac{1}{4}$. (825.)   PHILOCTETES.

SCOTT, DAVID.   VINTAGER.
45 × 37½. (342.)

SCOTT, DAVID.   PARACELSUS LECTURING.
57½ × 71½. (796.)

SCOTT, WILLIAM BELL.   ALBRECHT DÜRER OF NÜRNBERG.
23⅛ × 28¼.   (969.)

SCOUGALL, JOHN.

PORTRAIT OF THE PAINTER.
24 × 19.   (2032.)

SEGHERS. $11\frac{1}{8} \times 15\frac{3}{8}$.   (69.)   LANDSCAPE.

SETON, J. T.   LADY BARROWFIELD.
                        30×25.   (1840.)

L

TRIUMPHAL PROCESSION.

$16\frac{1}{4} \times 65\frac{1}{2}$. (1538.)

SELLAJO (attr.).

STORY FROM BOCCACCIO.

$15\frac{1}{2} \times 56$.   (1738.)

ROSSELLO DI JACOPO FRANCHI.

SELLAJO.　　　　　12½ × 18¼. (1941.)　　　　　MAN OF SORROWS.

SERODINE.　　　　　　　　　　　　　　　THE TRIBUTE MONEY.

57 × 89½. (1513.)

SIMSON, WILLIAM.   SOLWAY MOSS—SUNSET.

$25\frac{1}{4} \times 36\frac{1}{4}$.   (308.)

SISLEY, A. $17\frac{3}{4} \times 21\frac{3}{8}$.   (1775.)   EFFET DE NEIGE.

SNYDERS, FRANS.   MISCHIEVOUS MONKEYS.
$38\frac{1}{8} \times 45\frac{1}{4}$. (532.)

SOMERVILLE, ANDREW.   COTTAGE CHILDREN.
$14 \times 11\frac{7}{8}$. (805.)

SPANISH SCHOOL. $71\frac{1}{2} \times 36\frac{1}{8}$. (1021.)   ST. MICHAEL.

SPANISH SCHOOL (?).
CAVALIER IN YELLOW COAT.
$26\frac{7}{8} \times 21\frac{3}{4}$. (1728.)

STEEN, JAN.   PHYSICIAN AND PATIENT.
$27\frac{5}{8} \times 22\frac{1}{4}$. (86.)

SYME, J.   35½ × 27. (721.)
PORTRAIT OF REV. JOHN BARCLAY, M.D.

TERBRUGGHEN, H.   DECOLLATION OF S. JOHN.
                    66 × 85¾. (28.)

TENIERS, DAVID. PEASANTS PLAYING AT SKITTLES.
$13\frac{1}{8} \times 21\frac{3}{4}$. (90.)

THOMAS, J. H. CASTANETS.
$13\frac{3}{4}$ ins. high. (1615.)

THOMSON, REV. JOHN. $24\frac{5}{8} \times 36\frac{1}{2}$. (556.)   ABERLADY BAY.

THOMSON, REV. JOHN. $19\frac{1}{2} \times 29\frac{3}{4}$. (1727.)   FAST CASTLE.

THOMSON, REV. JOHN.   FAST CASTLE FROM BELOW.
$29\frac{1}{2} \times 41$. (2039.)

TIEPOLO. $26 \times 14\frac{3}{4}$. (91.)
ANTONY AND CLEOPATRA.

FINDING OF MOSES.

$77\frac{3}{4} \times 133\frac{3}{4}$.   (92.)

TIEPOLO, G. B.

TINTORETTO.   AUTUMN.
$45\frac{1}{4} \times 37\frac{1}{2}$. (96.)

TINTORETTO.   SUMMER.
$45\frac{1}{2} \times 37\frac{1}{2}$. (97.)

TRAQUAIR, MRS. PHOEBE ANNA.   TRIPTYCH.
Centre panel (frame), $8\frac{3}{4} \times 7\frac{1}{8}$.
Side panels, $8\frac{3}{4} \times 3\frac{5}{8}$.   (1871.)

TROYON, C.   UN PÂTURAGE EN TOURAINE.
$31 \times 45\frac{1}{2}$.   (1033.)

TURNER, J. M. W.   HEIDELBERG.
Water-colour, 14⅝ × 21¾. (885.)

TURNER, J. M. W.   DURHAM.
Water-colour, 11⅝ × 17¾. (883.)

TURNER, J. M. W.   SOMER HILL, TUNBRIDGE.
                    35 × 47.   (1614.)

TURNER, J. M. W.   Water-colour, 12¾ × 18½.   (884.)   LLANBERIS LAKE.

VELDE, WILLEM VAN DE. BOATS IN A CALM.
$15\frac{3}{4} \times 21\frac{3}{4}$ (114.)

VERMEER. $62\frac{1}{4} \times 55\frac{1}{4}$. (1670.)
CHRIST IN THE HOUSE OF MARTHA AND MARY.

M

VERONESE, PAOLO.   64¼ × 49¼. (339.)   MARS AND VENU

VRIES, A. DE.   SAMSON.

28 ins. high.   (137.)

VITALE DA BOLOGNA.   THE ADORATION OF THE MAGI.

$23\frac{1}{2} \times 15\frac{1}{4}$.   (952.)

WATTEAU, ANTOINE.   FÊTE CHAMPÊTRE.
$21\frac{1}{2} \times 17\frac{3}{4}$. (439.)

WATTEAU, ANTOINE.
FRENCH PASTORAL.
$9\frac{1}{4} \times 7\frac{1}{8}$. (370.)

WILKIE, SIR D. 23 × 42. (1527.) PITLESSIE FAIR.

WILKIE, SIR D. JOSEPHINE AND
THE FORTUNE TELLER.
83 × 62. (2114.)

WILKIE, SIR D.   THE GENTLE SHEPHERD.
$11\frac{5}{8} \times 15\frac{5}{8}$. (839.)

WILKIE, SIR DAVID.
THE LETTER OF INTRODUCTION.
$24 \times 19\frac{3}{4}$. (1890.)

WILKIE, SIR D.   38¼ × 48¼.   (1445.)   THE BRIDE'S TOILET.

WILKIE, SIR D.   47 × 62.   (2130.)   IRISH WHISKEY STILL.

WILKIE, SIR D. THE PAINTER.
$29\frac{1}{4}\times24$. (S.N.P.G. 573.)

WILSON, ANDREW. $11\frac{1}{4}\times17\frac{1}{4}$. (326.) VIEW OF TIVOLI.

WILSON, RICHARD.   RIVER SCENE, WITH FIGURES.
                    $33\frac{1}{4} \times 49\frac{1}{8}$. (620.)

WILSON, RICHARD. $20\frac{1}{4} \times 28\frac{3}{4}$. (331.)   ITALIAN LANDSCAPE.

WINGATE, SIR J. L.   A SUMMER EVENING.
                    $21\frac{3}{8} \times 29\frac{1}{4}$. (1649.)

WINGATE, SIR J. L. $34\frac{1}{2} \times 44\frac{1}{2}$. (2111.)   SHEEPSHEARING.

WINGATE, SIR J. L. $16\frac{7}{8} \times 12\frac{1}{4}$.   (1488.)

ASH TREES IN SPRING.

WINGATE, SIR J. L. $9\frac{3}{4} \times 13\frac{3}{4}$.   (2123.)   HARVEST IN ARRAN.

WINT, PETER DE.   THE HARVEST FIELD.
$12\frac{1}{2} \times 19\frac{1}{8}$. (1685.)

ZURBARAN.   IMMACULATE CONCEPTION.
$98\frac{3}{4} \times 67\frac{3}{4}$. (340.)

WINTOUR, J. C.   RIVERSIDE LANDSCAPE.
                    16½ × 23½.   (1489.)

WITTE, E. DE.   74¾ × 63¾.   (990.)
INTERIOR OF AMSTERDAM CATHEDRAL.

TINTORETTO. DRAWING after MICHELANGELO.
$13\frac{3}{8} \times 9\frac{5}{8}$. (R.N. 1853.)

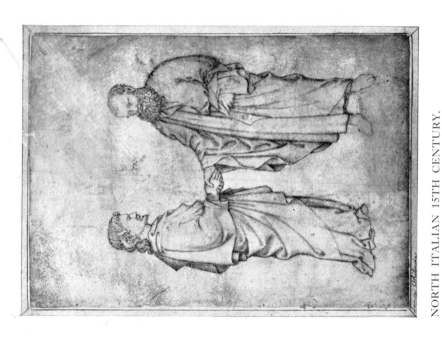

NORTH ITALIAN 15TH CENTURY. TWO SAINTS.
$7\frac{1}{4} \times 5\frac{1}{8}$. (R.N. 2259.)